-oOo-

Python Recipes for Engineers and Scientists

SCRIPTS THAT DEVOUR YOUR INTEGRALS,
EQUATIONS, DIFFERENTIAL EQUATIONS,
AND INTERPOLATIONS!

Javier Riverola Gurruchaga

To my wife and sons, Dolores, Javier and Diego, for their support and good advice

Contents

Introduction

Dear reader, this book is not a Python manual. It does not replace the many excellent books on the use of this cool language. There are tons of information on the Internet (tutorials, manuals, users groups, examples), so it is alive and accessible from any computer with connection to The Web[1]. Nor is it an exhaustive compendium of calculation options that covers the many possible problems with which an engineering student or professional is met.

What this book provides is a friendly help to some of the frequent numerical problems that arise in the analytical study of many engineering and physical problems. The chapters of the book get to the point in a simple way by deliberately renouncing to impress the reader with the ultra-power and sophistication of Python in favor of readability and comprehension. The included miniscripts are autonomous and solve very specific problems and the reader will see that they can be combined and adapted to real problems.

In a way, this is the cookbook that I would have liked to

---

[1]Good reference sites are http://www.Python.org, Python Programming in Wikibooks https://en.wikibooks.org/wiki/Main_Page, or the excellent books like "Automate the Boring Stuff with Python" by Al Sweigart.

have in my graduate and undergraduate courses and that I dare to write now after quite a few years of engineering work in which the quick solution of problems was a necessity and it remains so. Really, the simple and the practical is what remains after your being in trouble sometimes. For simplicity, I assumed that the reader has some basic knowledge of writing scripts: write a formula, create and manipulate arrays, plot simple graphs, import modules such as *numpy*, *scipy*, and *matplotlib*, ... although not necessarily advanced knowledge. It is not a book for specialists.

I have selected the topics ordered according to a postgraduate course in numerical methods (interpolation, differential equations, integration, etc.), avoiding all the theoretical apparatus and leaving only what is useful and essential, without entering into other topics such as optimization, treatment of images, creation of operating systems, etc. In addition to the recipes, the reader is challenged at the end of the book with some interesting exercises with the dual purpose of reviewing and escaping from boring life: identify a whale by singing, calculate pi with unorthodox methods, solve the Schrodinger equation, and so on.

Over many years I have tried different programming languages from Assembler, Fortran, Matlab / Octave, and the like, but I have found in Python a freshness and a dynamism very much in line with these times. It is even an element of free conversation with the new generation of professionals, for example with one of my sons, also an engineer, and friends. You may know that the Zen of Pyton is (Tim Peters[2]):

Beautiful is better than ugly.

---

[2]Easter egg: try in Python console >import this

Explicit is better than implicit.

Simple is better than complex.

Complex is better than complicated.

Readability counts.

I have enjoyed writing this book and I hope that you will also enjoy it and that it will be of benefit to you in your studies and professional life.

Javier Riverola

CONTENTS

1 | Interpolation and Fitting

There are many occasions in Engineering and Science in which it is necessary to interpolate an unknown y value for a given x among pairs of values (x_0, y_0),..., (x_n, y_n). For instance, this might be the case that we require a thermophysical property of a material (conductivity, density, ...) but we have only tables with a few pairs of values, or perhaps it might be the case that we need to estimate a credible result between actual results of a test or calculations, and that sort of things.

Interpolation is a kind of routine task but you ought to be careful to avoid unpleasant surprises. There is a suitable method of interpolation for each situation, depending on the risk that you want to assume, and on whether you can infer in advance some smooth or abrupt behavior, or on your knowledge of trends at the extremes of the interval of interpolation. We will explore some of these possibilities in this chapter.

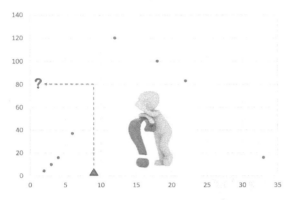

I wonder what the y value is!

1.1 Linear Interpolation

Linear interpolation is useful when, according to a conservative strategy, you do not want to take risks, even at the cost of giving up on obtaining a more accurate prediction. There are many cases in which this way of proceeding is the most appropriate.

The idea is quite simple: just find the interval i that contains the x value to interpolate, an draw a straight line passing through both extremes of the interval, so you can estimate the y value.

$$y \simeq f_i + (x - x_i)\frac{f_{i+1} - f_i}{x_{i+1} - x_i}$$

This is done easily in Python with:

```
y = interp(x, xdata, ydata)
```

We obtain the same result with:

```
y = float(interp1d(xdata, ydata,'linear')(x))
```

The latter form is more sophisticated, but more interesting because one can change easily from `'linear'` to `'quadratic'`, or `'cubic'`, as needed. The *Examples* subsection includes some of these options.

1.2   Pure Polynomial Interpolation

We search for a polynomial that passes thru all n+1 points,

$$y = a_0 + a_1 x + a_2 x^2 + ... + a_n x^n$$

so we can interpolate y$\simeq P_n(x)$.

We can write the linear system of equations as a matrix system:

$$\begin{bmatrix} 1 & x_0 & x_0^2 & ... & x_0^n \\ 1 & x_1 & ... & & x_1^n \\ \vdots & & & & \\ 1 & ... & & & x_n^n \end{bmatrix} \begin{Bmatrix} a_0 \\ \vdots \\ a_n \end{Bmatrix} = \begin{Bmatrix} y_0 \\ y_1 \\ \vdots \\ y_n \end{Bmatrix}$$

Now, we can obtain the unknown coefficients immediately as follows:

$$\{a\} = [X]^{-1} \cdot \{Y\}$$

However, this system is ill conditioned with both small and large number together and rounding errors may emerge and ruin the outcome. There is a number of popular techniques to calculate a_i without the need to solve the system such as the Newton's, Langrange's, and Aitken's interpolation methods.

But, we will bypass all them, and we will let Python do the job as follows:

```
y = poly1d(polyfit(xdata,ydata,len(xdata)-1))(x)
```

It seems tricky but it works. Besides, if you need the values of the polynomial coefficients, then just run:

```
c = polyfit(xdata, ydata, len(xdata)-1)
```
where c array is ordered from highest to lowest degree term $(a_n, ... a_0)$.

Warnings!

✏ *Pure polynomial may oscillate especially near extremes, and near to abrupt changes in data trends. For this rease, a polynomial larger than fifth degree is rarely used. If there are many data points, it is better to perform interpolations based on least squares fit or splines, as explained in next section.*

✏ *Besides, it is not recommended to use a pure polynomial for extrapolating purposes, that is, to obtain results out of the $[x_0, x_n]$ range. If you cannot escape from extrapolating, then you should perform a linear extrapolation instead.*

1.3   Cubic Splines

A spline is a differentiable curve defined in portions by polynomials. It is an interpolation method consisting of dividing the set of points into pieces ensuring continuity, which has many advantages and it has a correspondence with many physical phenomena. We can imagine a spline as a flexible and resistant rod that passes through each of the data points in a smooth manner.

Here, we are going to sketch only the most relevant spline formulation, which is the *cubic spline with continuous second derivative* (C^2). If our data points are $(x_0, y_0) \ldots (x_n, y_n)$, the spline is a cubic polynomial as shown below:

$$s(x) = A\frac{(x - x_j)^3}{h_j^3} + B + \frac{(x - x_j)^2}{h_j^2} + C\frac{(x - x_j)}{h_j} + D$$

where x_j is the lower end of the interval containing x, and $h_j = x_{j+1} - x_j$. Parameters A, B, C, and D are obtained by imposing conditions to the first derivative $S'(x)$ and second derivative $S''(x)$ to be the same at both sides of each data point. These conditions are applied to all points except the first and last ones, where boundary conditions are arbitrarily defined, so a system of equations is obtained.

Fortunately, Python includes the `scipy.interpolate` module that totally automatize the process:

```
y = float(interp1d(xdata, ydata,'cubic')(x))
```

A spline finds a good way!

1.4   Example of Interpolation Methods

This example shows the different methods that were described
above, applied to the same data set.

```
1  #
2  #       Interpolation Methods - Example
3  #
4
5  from numpy import array, poly1d, polyfit
6  from scipy.interpolate import interp1d
7
8  #    Your data
9  xdata = array([2,3,4,6,12,18,22,33,40,45,50,57])
10 ydata = array([4.5,10,16,37,120,
11                   100,83.9,65,64,66,70,71])
12
13 xv = 3.5  # value to interpolate
14
15 # Linear
16 yv_lin = interp1d(xdata, ydata,
17                   kind='linear')(xv)
18
19 # Pure polynomial
20 yv_pol = poly1d(polyfit(xdata, ydata,
21                   len(xdata)-1))(xv)
22
23 # Quadratic spline
24 yv_qspl = interp1d(xdata, ydata,
25                   kind='quadratic')(xv)
26
27 # Cubic spline
28 yv_cspl = interp1d(xdata, ydata,
29                   kind='cubic')(xv)
30
31 print("y_lin =",yv_lin,
```

```
32  "\ny_pol  =",yv_pol,
33  "\ny_qspl =",yv_qspl,
34  "\ny_cspl =",yv_cspl)
35
```

and the result is

```
y_lin  = 13.0
y_pol  = 12.7535196168
y_qspl = 13.188152688568351
y_cspl = 12.74574808523611
```

We can see in Figure 1.1 that results may differ greatly. The result at all nodes x_i is identical to the data y_i but different in between.

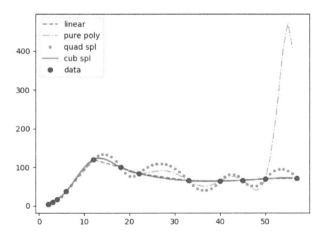

Figure 1.1: Think twice when choosing an interpolation method!. Here, linear or cubic splines are the best options.

17

1.5 Least Squares

The Least Squares (LS) method is not truly an interpolation method, but an artifice for smoothing and correcting experimental data. In addition, it provides a polynomial that fits the data in a consistent and smart way, and that can be used instead of the data itself as a formula, although it does not necessarily passes through all of them. It is a widely used tool in many engineering fields.

The first formulations of the method of least squares dates from 1805 (Legendre and Gauss), when the power of the predictive method was shown in situations where the observational data incorporate a certain degree of error.

Our goal is to find a polynomial $P_m = \sum_{i=0}^{m} a_i x^i$ of lesser degree than the pure polynomial, which passes near the points exhibiting a less oscillating behavior. Least square polynomials tend to compensate to some extent for intrinsic errors associated with data points. The $a_0, ... a_n$ coefficients are determined in such a way as to minimize the quadratic error of the fitting at all the points. In matrix form:

$$\begin{bmatrix} n+1 & \sum x_i & \sum x_i^2 & ... & \sum x_i^m \\ \sum x_i & \sum x_i^2 & ... & ... & \sum x_i^{m+1} \\ \sum x_i^2 & ... & ... & ... & \sum x_i^{m+2} \\ ... & & & & \\ \sum x_i^m & \sum x_i^{m+1} & ... & ... & \sum x_i^{2m} \end{bmatrix} \begin{Bmatrix} a_0 \\ a_1 \\ \vdots \\ a_m \end{Bmatrix} = \begin{Bmatrix} \sum y_i \\ \sum x_i y_i \\ \vdots \\ \sum x_i^m y_i \end{Bmatrix}$$

and solve for $\{a\}$. This system always has a solution, although with some caveats because small and very large quantities coexist in the same matrix. If we have n + 1 data points, and

- if m<n, the solution exists and it is unique.

- if m = n, the solution is a pure interpolation and it is unique.

- if m > n, there are infinite solutions.

Normally we have many n+1 points and use a small m-degree polynomial. The higher degree of the fitting polynomial, the closer to actual data points it runs. But keep in mind that we are not looking for a pure interpolation polynomial, but a softer, lower order polynomial, which does not oscillate, and that somehow compensates for inherent errors of the data.

As a suggestion, you can represent the points in a scatter plot. Afterwards, you can try a degree that is equal to the number of trend changes plus one, and then increase the degree of LS fit. A plot with all the cases can be of great help. Many authors indicate that the best fit is the one that results in a higher regression coefficient. However, the generalization of this criterion leads to the polynomial of pure interpolation, which by definition will give the maximum adjustment of 100% passing through all the points, but that is not what we are looking for. Instead, I recommend gradually increasing the degree of the LS regression polynomial, and plotting the result to observe the behavior, not only at the data but also in the intermediate intervals. In the example below, polynomial fit was increased to an 8th degree, but beyond that, the polynomial began to exhibit an oscillatory behavior.

```
1  #
2  #    Least Squares - Example
3  #
4
5  from numpy import array, poly1d, polyfit, arange
6  from scipy.interpolate import interp1d
7
8  #   My x data
9  xdata = array([2, 3, 4, 6, 12, 18, 22, 33, 40,
10                  45, 50, 57])
11
12  #   My y data
13  ydata = array([4.5, 10, 16,37,120,100, 83.9,65,
14                  64, 66, 70, 71])
15
16  #   Calculate all LS fits
17  a2 = polyfit(xdata, ydata, 2)
18  a3 = polyfit(xdata, ydata, 3)
19  a8 = polyfit(xdata, ydata, 8)
20
21  #   Finer x range just for plotting
22  xvals = arange(2,57,.5)
23  yvals_LST2 = poly1d(a2) (xvals)
24  yvals_LST3 = poly1d(a3) (xvals)
25  yvals_LST8 = poly1d(a8) (xvals)
26
27  #   Plot LS fits
28  import matplotlib.pyplot as plt
29  plt.close('all') # erase old plots
30  fig = plt.figure(1)
31  plt.plot(
32      xvals,yvals_LST2,'b-',
33      xvals,yvals_LST3,'r-',
34      xvals,yvals_LST8,'y-',
35      xdata,ydata,'bo')
36  plt.legend(('LS2','LS3','LS8','data'))
37
```

```
38 #    Print results
39 print('Coefficients are:',a8 )
```

```
Coefficients are:
[1.21242621e-09   -3.31174174e-07
 3.75413629e-05   -2.27553315e-03
 7.89102201e-02   -1.54036561e+00
 1.51737533e+01   -5.36623265e+016
 .55567161e+01]
```

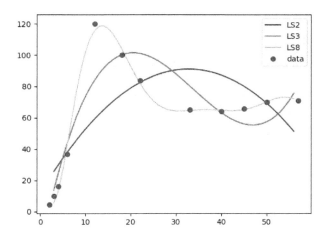

Figure 1.2: Least Squares Fit of data. LS8 fits well with no oscillation. Do not go further!

2 | Integration

2.1 Symbolic Integration

2.1.1 Symbolic Indefinite Integrals

Back in my early days of undergraduate student courses, solving integrals was a very entertaining challenge, and at the same time a sure question in the exams. There was a number of rules to find the primitive functions depending on whether the integrand was a polynomial, a rational function, trigonometric, all very tricky and uncertain. I could not imagine that there would come a day when such an artisan task could be solved with a computer with symbolic capacity.

The Plimpton table (1900 b.C.), Pythagorean triples $a^2 + b^2 = c^2$

The Python sympy module facilitates this task as can be seen in the examples that follow.

★ Let us assume that we want to obtain the primitive of

$$\int (6x^5 + \frac{log(x)}{x})dx$$

```
1 #    Symbolic Indefinite Integral example
2 from sympy import *
3
4 x = Symbol('x')
5
6 i1=integrate(6*x**5 + log(x)/x, x)
7
8 print('Result is ',i1)
9
```

```
Result is x**6 + log(x)**2/2
```

2.1.2   Symbolic Defined Integrals

★ Let us try something more sophisticated such as a symbolic definite integral expression. In this case we are combining reals with non rational and ordinal numbers.

$$\int_{-\pi/2}^{b} cos(x) + sin(x)dx + \int_{0}^{\infty} \frac{sin(x)}{\sqrt{x}}dx$$

```
1 #    Symbolic defined integral example
2
3 from sympy import *
4 from numpy import pi, inf
5
6 x = Symbol('x')
7 b = Symbol('b')
```

```
 8
 9  i2 = integrate(cos(x)+sin(x), (x, -pi/2, b)) +
        integrate(sin(x)/(x*0.5),(x, 0, inf))
10
11  print('Result is ',i2)
12
```

```
Result is   sin(b) - cos(b) + 4.14159265358979
```

Impressive!

2.2   Numerical Integration

2.2.1   Integrand is a formula

This is the most general case, in which the integrand is a mathematical expression and limits are given. In physics and engineering, it is common to calculate an extensive magnitude from an intensive magnitude (ie, mass from density), or to calculate the average of a property (i, e., conductivity, temperature ...), or perhaps to calculate an integral of a function over a multidimensional domain (area, moment of inertia,...).

In many cases, performing the integration manually is not easy and the availability of numerical methods is really helpful.The reader will discover in the following lines the ease and power of the method described in this section.

The `scipy.integrate` module includes different methods such as Gaussian and Romberg quadratures. However, we prefer quad routine, which is an implementation of the Fortran library QUADPACK for definite integrals.

★ Let us solve the following integral:

$$\int_0^3 \frac{e^{x-1}}{2x+1} dx$$

```
1  #    Integrand is a formula - Example
2
3  from scipy.integrate import quad
4  from scipy import exp
5
6  def Fun(x):
7      y = exp(x-1)/(2*x+1)
8      return y
9
10 I_quad = quad(Fun, 0,3)
11
12 print('Result is ',I_quad)
13
```

```
Result is   (1.5029081534735966, 7.638285955657406
    e-12)
```

Both the solution of the integral and the estimated error are given in the result array.

★ In this example, one of the limits of integration is infinity. Show that the result is π/2.

$$\int_0^\infty \frac{1}{x^2+1} dx = \pi/2$$

```
1  #    Improper Integral - Example
2
3  from scipy.integrate import quad
4  from numpy import inf
```

```
5
6 def Fun(x):
7     y = 1/(x*x+1)
8     return y
9
10 I = quad(Fun, 0,inf)
11
12 print('Result is',I)
13
14 # Exact result should be  pi/2
15
```

```
Result is (1.5707963267948966, 2.5777915205989877
    e-10)
```

Note that in the examples given above, functions were defined in a canonic way (def ... return). However, they can be written in a more compact equivalent manner:

```
Fun = lambda x:  1/(x*x+1)
```

★ You may also perform double and triple integrals as follows:

$$\int_{y=0}^{1} \left(\int_{x=0}^{2} xy^2 dx \right) dy$$

```
1 #    Double Integral - Example
2
3 from scipy.integrate import dblquad
4
5 f = lambda x,y: x*y**2
6 # note that x,y is the order of integration
7
8 I_box = dblquad(f, 0, 1, lambda x: 0, lambda x:
    2)
```

```
 9 # outer and inner limits. Inner are integrated
     first
10
11 print('Result is ',I_box)
12
```

```
Result is (0.6666666666666667, 2.2108134835808843
    e-14)
```

★ Even more, the limits can be variable expressions:

$$\int_{x=0}^{1} \int_{x=y}^{y^2+1} x^2 y \cdot dx dy$$

```
 1 #    Limits are Variable Expressions - Example
 2
 3 from scipy.integrate import dblquad
 4
 5 I_9 = dblquad(lambda x,y : x*x*y,
 6                 0, 1,
 7                 lambda y: y, lambda y: y*y+1)
 8 # Note that y,x are the same order as dx.dy
 9 # Note that limits order is outer and inner
10
11 print('Result is I_9 =',I_9)
12
```

```
Result is I_9 = (0.5583333333333333,
                 2.56811395902259e-14)
```

★ Yet, integrate with reverse order dydx :

$$\int_{x=0}^{1} \int_{y=0}^{e^x} \left(x + y^2 \right) \cdot dy dx$$

```
1  from scipy.integrate import dblquad
2
3  I_7 = dblquad(lambda y,x : x + y**2,
4                0, 1,
5                lambda x: 0, lambda x: exp(x))
6  # Note that y,x are the same order as dy.dx
7  # Note that limits order is outer and inner
8
9  print('Result is I_7 =',I_7)
10
```

```
Result is I_7 = (3.1206152136875187,
                 1.038969199265395e-13)
```

Certainly, the quad function is very powerful. You can perform all sort of simple, double, and triple integrals.

2.2.2 Montecarlo

The Montecarlo integration is an algorithm to estimate an approximation to a definite integral. The method consists of generating a large number of samples, where the integrand function is evaluated. The result is summed if the sample falls inside the integration domain. In the example below, we perform the Montecarlo integral of the last example in the previous section.

```
1  #   Montecarlo Integration - Example
2
3  from numpy import random, exp
4
5  x1, x2= 0, 1 # bounding box
6  y1, y2= 0, 4
7
8  # generate x,y samples
```

```
 9  n=5000 ; sum=0
10  x_sample = random.uniform(x1, x2, n)
11  y_sample = random.uniform(y1, y2, n)
12
13  for i in range(0,n):
14      x=x_sample[i]
15      y=y_sample[i]
16
17      # check if x,y inside bounds
18      if (y>0 and y< exp(x)):
19          inside = 1
20      else:
21          inside = 0
22
23      # accumulate function when inside
24      fun = x+y**2
25      sum = sum + fun*inside
26
27  I_montec=sum/n*(x2-x1)*(y2-y1)
28
29  print('I_Montecarlo = ',I_montec)
30
```

```
I_Montecarlo =  3.12422911458
```

Note that the result is an approximation to π=3.14159...

2.2.3 Integrand is pairs of data

In engineering, many circumstances arise in which, instead of an analytical function, only lists of pairs of values (x, y) are available. This is the normal case of tables of mechanical, thermophysical, or other properties. The integral can not be done with the previous methods and instead it is necessary to use the so-called *numerical quadratures*, in which the integral is replaced by a weighted sum:

$$\int_a^b [\{X\} \to \{Y\}] \cdot dx \simeq \sum_0^n w_i \cdot f(x_i)$$

Some quadratures are based on interpolation and others based on adaptive polynomials. Among the first, the most known and used are those of sum of rectangles by intervals, sum of trapezoids by intervals, Simpson's rule (polynomials of order 2 in equispaced points), Newton-Cotes quadratures (equispaced trapezoids), and Gaussian qua-dratures (with variable integration points). The use of these quadratures is appropriate when the *integration points or nodes* coincide with data, or when data are equispaced, but this is not always the case. Another difficulty that may arise is that the integration limits may not coincide with any of the known points x_i. In this section we propose to use a mixed method that exploits the power of Python with `scipy.integrate.quad` and `scipy.interpolate.splines`.

In the example below, we calculate the average density of vapor in a range of temperatures, assuming both linearity and splines for smoothness. Unless there are solid reasons to assume that the behavior is purely linear, it is more practical to assume that the transition is smooth and the spline method is the one that will give the most accurate results.

```
1  #    Integrate Arrays - Example
2
3  from scipy.integrate import quad
4  from scipy.interpolate import interp1d
5  from numpy import array
6
7  # Temperature of vapor, DC
```

```
 8  x1 = array([100,130,170,190,230,270,320,370])
 9
10  # Density of saturated steam, kg/m3
11  y1 = array([.598,1.496,4.122,6.397,
12        13.99,28.09,64.72,203.0])
13
14  # 1- Mean density asuming LINEARITY
15
16  I_lin = quad(lambda x: interp1d(x1, y1,'linear')(
        x),150,300)
17  Mean_lin = I_lin[0] /(300-150)
18
19  # 2- Mean density asuming SMOOTHNESS
20
21  I_splines = quad(lambda x: interp1d(x1, y1,'cubic
        ')(x), 150,300)
22  Mean_splines = I_splines[0] /(300-150)
23
24  print('Mean_lin=',Mean_lin,'kg/m3')
25  print('Mean_splines=',Mean_splines,'kg/m3')
26
```

```
Mean_lin= 17.30806667011904 kg/m3
Mean_splines= 16.230042258274562 kg/m3
```

Note that both results differ significantly. One must discern which method is more suitable according to the data type.

2.2.4   Fourier Transform

The integral known as the Fourier Transform deserves special attention for its applications in various branches of science. In the field of a time signal, this function decomposes a time function f(t) into its frequency components.

32

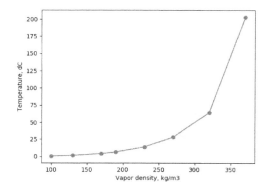

Figure 2.1: Data referring to Section 2.2.3. In this example, linear is fine, but smoothness (C2 continuity) looks a good assumption too!

$$\widehat{f}(\omega) = \frac{1}{\sqrt{2\pi}} \int_{-\infty}^{\infty} f(t)e^{i\omega t}$$

Normally, the time signal f(t) is a discrete sample so the *Discrete Fourier Transform* is applicable.

$$y_k = \sum_{n=0}^{n-1} exp\{-2\pi j \frac{kn}{N}\}f_n$$

In Python, all this is automatic so we call the `scipy.fftpack.fft` routine. One of the proposed problems in this book illustrates how to perform a Fourier analysis. Please refer to Section 6.5.

3 Solving equations

3.1 Systems of Linear Equations

Systems of linear equations or linear systems are well known to all students from high school and college courses, and they frequently break into a multitude of engineering fields. There are many coupled physical systems that ideally obey linear laws. Therefore linear systems are a fundamental framework that we must handle many times.

$$
\begin{bmatrix}
a_{00} & a_{01} & \dots & a_{0n} \\
a_{10} & a_{11} & \dots & a_{1n} \\
\vdots & & & \\
a_{n0} & a_{n1} & \dots & a_{nn}
\end{bmatrix}
\begin{Bmatrix}
x_0 \\
\vdots \\
x_n
\end{Bmatrix}
=
\begin{Bmatrix}
y_0 \\
y_1 \\
\vdots \\
y_n
\end{Bmatrix}
$$

There are many methods of solution: row reduction, elimination of variables, matrix solution, Gaussian elimination, ... Examples appear even in the user manuals of use of hand calculators.

This book includes a self-explanatory example of the use of the coefficient matrix with two methods:
The numpy.linalg.solve library and by matrix inverse.

```
1  #    System of linear equations
2
3  from numpy import array,matmul
4  from numpy import linalg
5
6  my_matrix = array([[1, 2, 5 ,6],
7                     [4, -4 ,-6, 8],
8                     [-12, 1, 3, 9],
9                     [18, 0, 0, 6]])
10
11 my_vector = array( [1, 6, 7 , 2])
12
13 solution = linalg.solve(my_matrix,my_vector)
14
15 print('Solution is x1, x2, x3, x4 =',solution)
16
17 # Alternate method
18 solution1 = matmul(linalg.inv(my_matrix),
       my_vector)
19
20 print('Solution is x1,x2,x3,x4 by inv[A]*b =',
       solution1)
21
```

```
Solution is x1, x2, x3, x4 =
[-0.18245614  3.27368421 -2.12982456  0.88070175]

Solution is x1,x2,x3,x4 by inv[A]*b =
[-0.18245614  3.27368421 -2.12982456  0.88070175]
```

Of course, both solutions are identical.

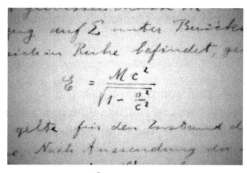

First occurrence of $E = mc^2$ by A. Einstein. Photo by Peat Bakke

3.2   Systems of non-linear Equations

Sooner or later, engineers and scientists encounter one or more
nonlinear equations whose solution is not immediate because
the unknown variables can not be cleared and the solution can
not be obtained easily by substitution or another direct method.
In these cases we can follow an iterative method in which we
start with a first guess and then we approach the solution by
successive approximations.

   The most well-known methods to find solutions by successive approximations of a non-linear equation or system are
fixed-point iteration, the *secant method*, and the *Newton-Raphson
method*. The later is described next.

3.2.1   Newton-Raphson

Let $f(x) = 0$ be an equation that we need to solve.
   After linearization, this equation becomes

$$f(x_0) + f'(x_0)(x - x_0) \simeq 0$$

Now, variable x can be cleared to as the iterative formula.

$$x_{n+1} \simeq x_n - \frac{f(x_n)}{f'(x_n)}$$

In this book we recommend to use the scipy.optimize.fsolve routine, which is actually based on the Newton's method. In the example below we solve a truly devilish non-linear system.

```
1  #    System of NON-linear equations
2
3  from scipy.optimize import fsolve
4  from numpy import sqrt
5
6  def Equations(p):
7      x,y,z,t,u,v = p
8
9      # Equations writen as F(x)=0
10     err1 = (x**2 + 2)/sqrt(y) - 1.1
11     err2 = x*y/2 - 15
12     err3 = y - 4 + z*t**2
13     err4 = x + y + z/t
14     err5 = (x*y - z*t)*u
15     err6 = v - 30
16
17     #print(err1,err2,err3,err4,err5,err6)
18     return err1, err2, err3, err4, err5, err6
19
20 x,y,z,t,u,v = fsolve(Equations,[1,1,1,1,1,1])
21
22 print('Solution is x,y,z,t,u,v =',x,y,z,t,u,v)
23
```

```
Solution is x,y,z,t,u,v =
    1.64320097451 18.257048567  -17.8066500834
    0.894795316054 2.33469435623e-10 30.0
```

Note that `fsolve` needs to start the iteration from a first guess, which is [1,1,1,1,1,1] in this example. Besides, in order to know the error of each equation at the end of the iterative process, you may remove the comment character in line 17. If the NR method enters zero derivative in some iteration, try another initial point and take advantage of the `fsolve` automatism.

3.2.2   The Secant Method

Although the Newton-Raphson method is the preferred in most occasions, it may result in error if there is an inflexion, where derivative is zero or very small value. In these situations, it is advisable the use of secant method, which is essentially Newton-Raphson by replacing derivatives by secant.

The recurrence formula is:

$$x_{n+1} = x_n - f(x_n)\frac{x_n - x_{n-1}}{f(x_n) - f(x_{n-1})}$$

The secant method needs two starting values, x_0 and x_1, and avoids the evaluation of the derivatives. Coding is not complicated, there are many examples on the internet.

4   Differential Equations

Differential equations are of great import-
ance in science and engineering, because
many physical laws and relations appear
mathematically in the form of differential
equations. There are homogeneous and
non-homogeneous, linear and non-linear,
ordinary and partial derivatives differential equations.

4.1   Ordinary Differential Equations

It is a differential equation with only one
independent variable, usually time. In order to solve a set of ordinary diferential
equations, you write it in the form

"An equation has
no meaning for
me unless it ex-
presses a thought
of God". Srinivasa
Ramanujan

$$y^{(n)} = F(t, y, y^{(1)}, ..., y^{(n-1)})$$

The study of ordinary differential equations and their solution is a matter of entire courses at the university. It is a complete discipline of Calculus where it is approached with different techniques such as direct integration, separation of variables, linearization, Fourier series, and Laplace transforms. In this book the scipy.integrate.odeint numerical method is used, which relies in lsoda from the general FORTRAN library odepack.

⋆ Integrate ODE from 0 to 15, starting in x=2, y=3 (Note that the ODE includes a non-linear term).

$$\dot{x} = x - y + \frac{xy}{1000}$$

$$\dot{y} = 6x - 2y + 9$$

```
# 	System of Differential Equations - Example

from scipy.integrate import odeint

from numpy import arange

# set a time scale
t = arange(0,15,0.1)

# 	Define ODE system
def derivatives(state,t):
    x,y = state
    x_dot = x - y + 2 + x*y/100
    y_dot = 6*x - 2*y + 9
    return [x_dot, y_dot]

# 	Solve the ODE system
solution_x_y = odeint(derivatives, [2,3],t)
```

```
20 #    Unpack variables x and y
21 x = solution_x_y[:,0]
22 y = solution_x_y[:,1]
23
24 #    Draw phase plot and run plot
25 import matplotlib.pyplot as plt
26
27 plt.close('all')
28
29 fig = plt.figure(1)
30 plt.plot(x[0],y[0],'o',x,y,'r')
31
32 plt.title('Phase Diagram')
33 plt.xlabel('x')
34 plt.ylabel('y')
35 plt.legend(('start','run'))
36
37 fig = plt.figure(2)
38 plt.plot(t,x,'--',t,y)
39 plt.title('x and versus time')
40 plt.xlabel('time, s')
41 plt.ylabel('x and y')
42 plt.legend(('x','y'))
43
```

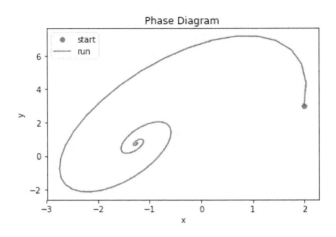

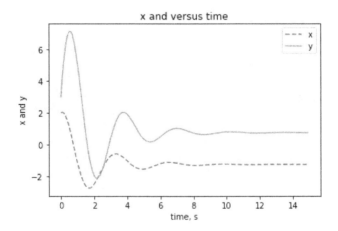

4.2   Partial Differential Equations

Laws of conservation of mass, energy, momentum, and other magnitudes such as electric charge, probability, stress and strain, are normally described with partial differential equations (PDE). What makes PDE very special is that the solution depends on the space, and possibly on time, i.e. multiple independent variables.

There are elliptical equations (for example the Laplace and Poisson equations), parabolic equations (heat equation), and hyperbolic equations (wave equation) and are conditioned or prescribed by a series of Dirichlet or Newmann type boundary conditions.

To solve differential equations in partial derivatives with numerical methods there are several techniques: finite differences, finite elements, finite volumes, ... In this book only an example of the first method is given, since the other two are beyond the scope of this book due to their complexity.

4.2.1   Finite Differences

Let us illustrate the method with a simple exercise. We want to solve the Laplace equation in a squared geometry which is 16x16 cm. The boundary conditions are: 20ºC along west and south borders, 250 ºC along north, and no heat transfer (adiabatic) at the east border.

$$\frac{\partial^2 T}{\partial x^2} + \frac{\partial^2 T}{\partial y^2} = 0.$$

After replacing space derivatives by finite differences, the equation above becomes:

$$\frac{T_{i+1,j} - 2T_{i,j} + T_{i-1,j}}{(\Delta x)^2} + \frac{T_{i+1,j} - 2T_{i,j} + T_{i-1,j}}{(\Delta y)^2} = 0$$

Here the central scheme is used, it can be generalized to any differentiation scheme.

```
1  #     Partial Differential Equations - Example
2
3  from numpy import meshgrid, arange, full
4
5  #    Build a mesh
6  X, Y = meshgrid(arange(0, 50),
7  arange(0, 50))
8
9  #    Initialize
10 U0 = 30 # first guess
11 U=full((50, 50), U0, dtype=float)
12
13 #    Boundary contitions
14 Unorth = 80
15 Usouth = 20
16 Uwest = 20
17 Ueast = 0
18
19 U[49:,:] =   Unorth       # Dirichlet
20 U[:1,:] =   Usouth       # Dirichlet
21 U[:, :1] =   Uwest        # Dirichlet
22 U[:, 49:] = Ueast ; U[:, 48] = Ueast    # Neumann
23
24 #    Iterate
25 ii=0
26 dxy = 1
27 while ii < 200:
28     for i in range(1, 49, dxy):
29         for j in range(1, 49, dxy):
30             U[i, j] = (U[i-1,j] + U[i+1,j] + U[i,
      j-1] + U[i,j+1])/4
31         ii+=1
32 U[:, 48] = Ueast
33
```

```
34 #    Contour plot of the solution U(x,y)
35 import matplotlib.pyplot as plt
36 plt.contourf(X, Y, U, 25, cmap=plt.cm.jet)
37 plt.colorbar()
38 plt.show()
39
```

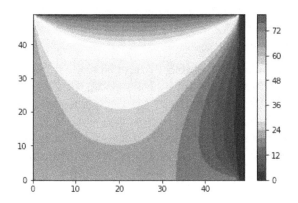

Temperature distribution in the plate, ºC

4.2.2   Finite Elements and Finite Volumes

The finite difference method described above currently has a more academic than practical utility. There are formulations in finite differences that try to contemplate non regular geometries but with little success. Currently, advanced numerical methods such as the Finite Element Method (FEM) and the Finite Volume Method (FVM) are used in engineering. Although both methods are applicable to any system of differential equations in multi-physical partial derivatives, the use of FEM is more consolidated for problems of structural analysis, elastic field and heat transfer, while FVM takes advantage of Gauss theorem to simplify integral equations when possible to apply, and is more dedicated to fluid mechanics (Navier Stokes). There are formulations of both types for the Maxwell equations, gravitational field, etc.

A detailed description of these methods is out of the scope of this introductory book, and the reader is invited to explore the capabilities of Python applications that use this type of numerical methods.

- **FEniCS.** The FEniCS Project Version 1.5 M. S. Alnaes, J. Blechta, J. Hake, A. Johansson, B. Kehlet, A. Logg, C. Richardson, J. Ring, M. E. Rognes and G. N. Wells Archive of Numerical Software, vol. 3, 2015, [DOI] Automated Solution of Differential Equations by the Finite Element Method A. Logg, K.-A. Mardal, G. N. Wells et al. Springer, 2012. See

  ```
  https://fenicsproject.org/
  ```

- **SfePy**. R. Cimrman. SfePy - write your own FE application. In P. de Buyl and N. Varoquaux, editors, Proceedings of the 6th European Con- ference on Python in Science (EuroSciPy 2013), pages 65–70, 2014.

  ```
  http://arxiv.org/abs/1404.6391.
  ```

- **FiPy.** J. E. Guyer, D. Wheeler and J. A. Warren, "FiPy: Partial Differential Equations with Python," Computing in Science and Engineering 11 (3) pp. 6-15 (2009). See

  ```
  https://www.nist.gov/publications/
  finite-volume-pde-solver-using-python-fipy
  ```

5   Mathematical Statistics

Whenever we perform an experiment in which we observe some quantity (strength, number of defects, weight of people,etc.) there is associated a random variable *xdata*. In Statistics we draw conclusions about the population from properties of samples . We do this by calculating point estimates, confidence intervals, upper and lower bounds, inferring a fitting distribution, and other relevant parameters.

Cora Ratto de Sadosky

In these lines, we will just tiptoe around a few essentials in this matter. For advanced use, Python libraries provide a very complete suite of functions, tests, and routines to deal with almost any need for the statistics researcher.

5.1   Mean and Standard Deviation

Mean and variance of a sample are defined by

$$\bar{x} = \frac{1}{n} \sum_{j=1}^{n} x_j$$

$$s^2 = \frac{1}{n-1} \sum_{j=1}^{n} (x_j - \bar{x})^2$$

Standard deviation is just the square root of variance.

Both sample mean $\bar{x}$, and sample variance s^2, are *point estimates* of the population mean μ, and population variance σ^2.

```
1  #    Sample Statistics - Example
2
3  from statistics import *
4
5  #    Sample data
6  xdata = [10.7, 10.9, 8.6,   8.2, 11.8, 9.9, 6.6,
7           9.8, 10.1,  10.1, 9.8, 12.3, 8.5, 12.1,
8           11.0, 9.2, 9.2, 7.1, 11.8, 6.0, 14.2,
9           10.0, 13.1, 9.0, 11.6, 9.6,  8.5, 10.2,
10          9.1, 9.3, 7.5, 10.2, 10.2, 9.6, 8.0,
11          11.8, 9.7,  7.3, 8.2, 10.0, 10.5, 11.1,
12          9.1,10.2, 7.5,  11.3, 9.8, 7.9, 8.4,
13          6.8, 7.0, 12.4, 8.9,  7.0, 9.8,  10.4,
14          10.0,   9.3,    10.0 ]
15
16 #    Sample parameters
17 x_sample = mean(xdata)
18 s_sample = stdev(xdata)
19 n = len(xdata)
20
21 print('Results are: ')
22 print('x_sample =',x_sample)
23 print('s_sample =',s_sample)
```

```
24  print('n =',n)
25
26  #    Plot histogram
27  import matplotlib.pyplot as plt
28  plt.hist(xdata)
29  plt.title("Histogram of xdata")
30  plt.xlabel("Value")
31  plt.ylabel("Frequency")
32
```

```
Results are:
x_sample = 9.63050847457627
s_sample = 1.6984023158989985
n = 59
```

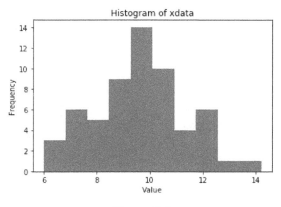

Figure 5.1

5.2   Confidence Limits of μ and σ^2

In general, the point estimates of the population mean and variance are not sufficient, and it is desired to estimate each parameter within a range that covers a high percentage of the possible values. These are the *Confidence Limits*. Assuming that our data come from a Normal distribution,

$$\bar{x} - t_{\frac{\alpha}{2}} \frac{s}{\sqrt{n}} \le \mu \le \bar{x} + t_{\frac{\alpha}{2}} \frac{s}{\sqrt{n}}$$

$$\frac{(n-1)s^2}{\chi^2_{\frac{\alpha}{2}}} \le \sigma^2 \le \frac{(n-1)s^2}{\chi^2_{1-\frac{\alpha}{2}}}$$

where t and χ^2 are the Student and Chi2 distributions, and α is the *significance level* (probability of taking a bad decision), typically 5 %.

```python
# ... continuation of the script above

from scipy.stats import t, chi2
from numpy import sqrt

# significance level
alpha = 0.05

# Confidence intervals for the pop. mean
tstudent=t.ppf(1-alpha/2,n-1)
mu_max = x_sample + tstudent*s_sample/sqrt(n)
mu_min = x_sample - tstudent*s_sample/sqrt(n)

# Confidence interval for the population std dev
Smin = sqrt((n-1)*s_sample**2/chi2.ppf(1-alpha/2,
    n-1))
Smax = sqrt((n-1)*s_sample**2/chi2.ppf(alpha/2,n
    -1))

print('Confidence Intervals are:')
print(mu_min,' <= mu <=',mu_max)
print(Smin,' <= Sigma2 <=',Smax)
```

```
21 print('\nwith significance level alpha=',alpha)
22 print('Confidence level gamma = 1-alpha =',1-
      alpha)
23
```

```
Confidence Intervals are:
9.18790242067   <= mu <= 10.0731145285
1.43775470204   <= Sigma2 <= 2.07536904664

with significance level alpha= 0.05
Confidence level gamma = 1-alpha = 0.95
```

5.3   Population Bounds

Another very useful quantity in statistical inference is the value
that covers a given percentage (say 95%) of all possible population values. This is the so-called **upper bound**.

If you knew the exact values of μ and σ of the population,
it would suffice to calculate the upper bound as $x_{95\%} = \mu +
1.645\sigma$. But these values are unknown. Instead, starting from
the known sample values, $\bar{x}$ and s, the upper bound value can
also be estimated with Owen's distribution,

$$x_{95\%} \simeq \bar{x} + k_{95\%} \cdot s$$

```
1 # ... Continuation of script above
2
3 #    Estimation of the 95/95 upper bound of the
      population
4
5 owen2 = lambda n: 1.96 + 2.1758/sqrt(n)+5.7423/n
```

53

```
 6
 7 owen1 = lambda n: 1.6449+2.4417/sqrt(n)+3.8171/n
 8
 9 up95_1tail = x_sample + owen1(n)*s_sample
10
11 up95_2tail = x_sample + owen2(n)*s_sample
12
13 print('Upper bounds of the population are:')
14 print('Up95_1tail =',up95_1tail,': 5% at right')
15 print('Up95_2tail =',up95_2tail,': 2.5% at right
       and left')
16
```

```
Upper bounds of the population are:
Up95_1tail = 13.0739832898 : 5% at right
Up95_2tail = 13.6057756047 : 2.5% at right and
    left
```

5.4   Test for a Distribution

Using a sample $x_1, ..., x_n$, we want to test the hypothesis that
a certain function F(x) is the distribution function from which
the sample was taken. There is a number of different tests. Currently, the recommended ones are Shapiro-Wilk (only check for
Normality) and Anderson-Darling tests, both described below.

54

5.4.1   Shapiro-Wilk Normality Test

```
1 # ... Continuation of script above
2
3 # Shapiro-Wilk Normality test
4
5 from scipy.stats import shapiro
6
7 sw = shapiro(xdata)
8
9 print('Shapiro-Wilks Test p=',sw[1],' W=',sw[0])
10 print('If p < w, do not reject Normality')
11
```

```
Shapiro-Wilks Test
p= 0.7642765641212463  W= 0.9866541028022766
If p < w, do not reject Normality
```

Interpretation: we do not reject the hypothesis that the sample comes from a normal distribution.

5.4.2   Anderson-Darling Test

```
1 # ...Continuation of script above
2
3 # Anderson Darling test
4
5 from scipy.stats import anderson
6
7 AD=anderson(xdata,dist='norm')
8
9 print(AD)
```

```
AndersonResult(statistic=0.32591792120113894,
critical_values=array([ 0.543,  0.619,  0.742,
    0.866,  1.03 ]),
significance_level=array([ 15. ,  10. ,  5. ,
    2.5,  1. ]))
```

Interpretation: since 0.3259 is lower than critical value 0.742, the hypothesis of normality is not rejected at 5% significance level.

6 │ Proposed Exercises

6.1 Complex Pendulum

Let us assume that we have a ruler is hanging from a hole near one extreme and we leave it to oscillate like a pendulum. Please, calculate the oscillating period by solving the differential equation of motion.

Data: Length L=0.46 m, mass m=0.180 kg, distance of the hole to extreme x=0.180 m, and initial angle θ=45 deg

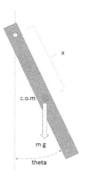

Figure 6.1

$$\frac{d^2\theta}{dt^2} = -\frac{mgx}{I_0}sin(\theta)$$

being $I_0 = mL^2/12 + mx^2$, the moment of inertia of the rule.

Sugestions:

- Asume $d\theta/dt = \phi$ to set a system of two first order differential equations

- You may use `scipy.integrate.odeint`

- Initial conditions are $\phi(0) = 0$ and $\theta(0) = \pi/4$

- Once you have solved the system, you may plot θ versus time, and calculate the period as the interval between two peaks.

- You can check your result by comparing with the analytical solution $T = 2\pi\sqrt{\frac{I_0}{mgx}}$

6.2 Pressure Drop in a Pipe

We have measured the pressure drop in a pipe ΔP=1000 N/m2. Obtain the mass flow rate m, assuming the equations given below. Data: the pipe diameter is D = 0.190 m, pipe length L = 2m, water temperature is T=20 °C (viscosity is 1004e-6, density ρ=0.998 kg/m3).

$$\Delta P = f_D \frac{L}{D} \rho \left(\frac{\dot{M}}{A\rho} \right)^2$$

$$\frac{1}{\sqrt{f_D/4}} = 4 log_{10} \left[\frac{Re\sqrt{F_D/4}}{1.255} \right]$$

$$Re = \frac{\dot{M}D}{A\mu}$$

Sugestions:

- You may use `scipy.optimize.fsolve`

- You may need to try with various *first guess.*

6.3   The Butterfly Effect

The butterfly effect appears for the first time in the science fiction tale *The Thunder* of Bradbury in 1952, which illustrates that in certain circumstances a small variation to the initial conditions can have great consequences in the medium or long term. It is one of the paradigms of chaos theory. In 1963, Edward Lorenz developed an

atmospheric model of oscil-
lating solution known as the Lorenz attractor. It was found by
chance that for certain combinations of σ (Prandtl number),
and ρ (Rayleigh number), the oscillations of the attractor lead
to chaotic behavior. In addition, the trajectories describe butterfly wings, so it has become the perfect example to illustrate
this effect.

$$\dot{x} = \sigma(y - x)$$
$$\dot{y} = x(\rho - z) - y$$
$$\dot{z} = xy - \beta z$$

It is proposed to solve the set of Lorenz equations with a
chaotic configuration; try $\sigma = 10$, $\rho = 28$ and $\beta = 8/3$ from t
= 0 to t = 200 seconds, starting from the point [0.0, 0.0001,
0.0] with a sufficiently small time step of 0.1 sec or 0.05 sec,
to be able to represent trajectories of x, y, z and observe the
appearance of wings.

In addition, it is proposed to return to solve the system starting from a very close point [0.0, 0.0002, 0.0], and see that the
trajectories are at first indistinguishable but beyond 30 seconds
they move away from each other and go every way they wish.

Sugestions:

- It is an ODE system. You may use
  `scipy.integrate.odeint`

- You may plot the trajectories in a 3D with
  `mpl_toolkits.mplot3d.Axes3D`

6.4   "Out of the Box"

Time independent Schrodinger equation is the following one:

$$-\frac{\hbar}{2m}\frac{d^2\psi}{dx^2} + v \cdot \psi = E \cdot \psi$$

where ψ is the wave function or the probability to find a particle, x is the space dimension, m is the mass of the particle, E is the kinetic energy, V is the heigth of the potential barrier, and $\hbar$ is the Plank´s constant.This equation is the basis to analyze the steady

"I insist upon the view that all is waves".   E. Schrodinger

states of atomic systems, and in certain circumstances, there is solution only for specific (quantified) energy states. Direct analytic solution is not a trivial issue but numerical methods allow you to obtain approximate solutions to a variety of scenarios.

If we replace $x \to x_j$,
$\psi \to \psi_j$,
$V \to V_j$,
$\frac{d^2\psi}{dx^2} \simeq \frac{\psi_{j+1} - 2\psi_j + \psi_{j-1}}{\Delta x^2}$,
we obtain:

$$\psi_{j+1} = \left[2 - \Delta x^2 \frac{2m}{\hbar}(E_j - V_j)\right]\psi_j - \psi_{j-1}$$

In order to work in more comfortable units, this equation becomes

$$\psi_{j+1} = \left[2 - \Delta x^2 \frac{2m}{\hbar} 1.362 \cdot 10^{-28} (E_j - V_j) \right] \psi_j - \psi_{j-1}$$

where m is the atomic mass in uma, E and V are given in electron-volt, and x is the distance in Armstrong.

The proposed problem is the following: assume an electron is inside a box with a potential barrier of 20 electron-volt between 2 and 3 Armstrong. Before and after this barrier, the potential is just zero.

x < 2 A	V = 0 eV
$2 \leq x \leq 3$ A	V = 20 eV
x > 3 A	V= 0 eV

Please find one or more energy levels for this electron inside the box and the associated wave function.

Take mass of electron m = 5.48e-4 uma and $\hbar$=6.58e-16 eV.s

The boundary conditions are: $\frac{d\psi}{dx} = 0$, and ψ=0 in a remote point, por instance x=6 A.

Suggested method:

1. Generate a large number of x nodes, say 601

2. Asume a guess value for E, and ψ(0)=ψ(1)=E, that is, the same value in order to force the zero gradient condition. This E guess value is irrelevant, because we will normalize the wave function later, but is necessary to start the iteration.

3. Calculate V_j for all nodes

4. Calculate $\psi(j)$ from j=2 to n

5. We will see that that ψ(n) at the last node will be not zero. Now, you can change E guess manually or with an automatic iterative process until you get ψ(n)=0. Then, you have to normalize the wave function:

$$\int_{-\infty}^{+\infty} |\psi(x)|^2 = 1$$

With Python this is immediate $\psi=\psi$/sum($\psi \cdot \psi$)**0.5

6. Plot the probability function, pdf = $\psi \cdot \psi$. Note that the probability function and wave function are not zero beyond the barrier. This result is not possible in classic mechanics, but it is in quantum mechanics.

6.5   Listen to that whale!

On the Internet you will find a lot of interesting sounds. In this exercise we propose to generate a script for the spectral analysis of a sound recorded in a .wav file by means of a Fourier analysis, actually with a Fast Fourier Transform.

A curious sound you can obtain is the song of the humpback whales. The reader is invited to download the file *"whale1.wav"*, available on the NOAA (National Oceanic and

Atmospheric Administration) website or simply by entering said name in Google and perform search. After analysing the record, two peaks will be obtained at 717 Hz and 915 Hz.

Other curious sounds are *"LaughingChild.wav"* (a child's laugh), *"rwbl10.wav"* (singing blackbird), and *"thunder3.wav"* (a stormy thunder!). All these and many others can be found easily on the Internet.

Sugestions:

1. Download a wav file

2. Read the sound file (data=wavfile.read(filein))

3. Perform a FFT analysis

4. Discard 2nd half

5. Plot the spectrum

6.6   Calculate π with Montecarlo

Now, some fresh air! Let us calculate number π with a Montecarlo integration. We know that the area inside a circle of radius r=1 is just the number π. Therefore, the reader may perform the following integral, being Ω a circle of prescribed radius.:

$$\iint_\Omega dx \cdot dy$$

Sugestions:

- Run a Montecarlo integration inside a box of sides x[-1 to 1] and y[-1 to 1]

- Compute success if $x^2 + y^2 < 1$

7 | Answers to Problems

7.1 Answer to *Complex Pendulum*

```python
# -*- coding: utf-8 -*-
"""
Created on Tue Feb 20 17:51:05 2018

Anwser to Complex Pendulum

"""
from scipy.integrate import odeint
from numpy import *

# --------------- data ------------------

L = 0.46
m = 0.042
x = 0.18
g = 9.81
I0 = m*(L**2/12) + m*x**2

# ---------------- calculations -------

t = arange(0,5,0.05)
```

```
22
23 def derivadas(state,t):
24
25     psi,theta = state
26     psi_dot = -m*g*x*sin(theta)/I0
27
28     theta_dot = psi
29     return [psi_dot, theta_dot]
30
31 soluciones = odeint(derivadas, [0,pi/4],t)
32 psi=soluciones[:,0] ; theta=soluciones[:,1]
33
34 # ------------- Plot results ------------
35
36 import matplotlib.pyplot as plt
37
38 plt.close('all') # Erase previous plots
39 fig = plt.figure(1)
40 plt.plot(t,theta,t,psi)
41 plt.legend(('Theta','Psi'))
42 plt.title('Complex Pendulum')
43 plt.xlabel('time, s')
44 plt.ylabel('Psi, theta, rad')
```

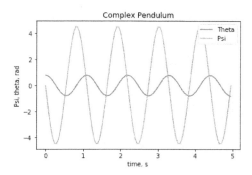

Figure 7.1: Note that the interval between two peaks is 1.1 sec. It is the same time as calculated with the anlytical period formula.

7.2 Answer to *Pressure Drop in a Pipe*

```python
from scipy.optimize import fsolve
from numpy import sqrt,log10

# ----- Data ------------------------

deltap = 1000
D = 0.10
L = 2;
mu = 1004e-6
rho = 998
A=0.00785

# ----- Solving the equations -------

def ecuations(p):

Mdot,fd,Reynolds = p

err1= deltap - (1/2)*fd*(L/D)*rho*(Mdot/(A*rho))
```

```
        **2
20  err2 = 1/sqrt(fd/4) - 4*log10(Reynolds*sqrt(fd/4)
        /1.255)
21  err3 = Reynolds - Mdot*D/(A*mu)
22  return err1, err2, err3
23
24  x,y,z = fsolve(ecuations,(10,0.01,100000))
25
26  # ----- Print the solution -----------------
27
28  print('Solution is:')
29  print('Mdot =', x)
30  print('fd = ',y)
31  print('Re =',z)
```

```
Solution is:
Mdot = 20.3260787498
fd =  0.0148854732663
Re = 257899.342119
```

7.3 Answer to *The Butterfly Effect*

```
1  # -*- coding: utf-8 -*-
2  """
3  Created on Tue Feb 20 17:51:05 2018
4
5  This script obtains a solution to the Lorentz
        attractor
6
7  Python 3.6.0
8
9  @author: jrg
10  """
11  from numpy import *
12  from scipy.integrate import quad, odeint
```

```python
13  import matplotlib.pyplot as plt
14
15  # ----- Data -----
16
17  sigma = 10
18  rho = 28
19  beta = 8/3
20  t = arange(0,200,0.05)
21
22  # ----- Calculations -----
23
24  def derivadas(estado,t):
25  x,y,z = estado
26  xdot = sigma*(y-x)
27  ydot = x*(rho - z)-y
28  zdot = x*y - beta*z
29
30  return [xdot, ydot, zdot]
31
32  soluciones = odeint(derivadas, [0,0.0001,0],t)
33  x=soluciones[:,0] ; y=soluciones[:,1] ; z =
        soluciones[:,2]
34
35  # ----- Results -----
36
37  from mpl_toolkits.mplot3d import Axes3D
38  plt.close('all')
39  fig = plt.figure(1)
40  ax = plt.axes(projection='3d')
41  ax.plot(x,y,z)
```

7.4   Answer to *"Out of the Box"*

```python
1  # -*- coding: utf-8 -*-
2  """
3  Created on Thu Feb  1 11:12:03 2018
```

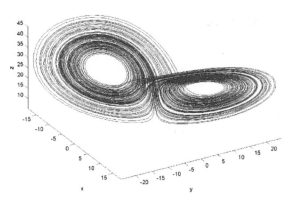

Figure 7.2: Here, the solution of the Lorentz attractor deploys as butterfly wings. This plot is extremely sensitive to very small departure from the initial condition.

```
4
5  Script to calculate the solution of the
      Schrodinger equation in a box
6
7  @author: jrg
8  """
9
10 from numpy import *
11 from scipy.optimize import fsolve
12
13 global f
14
15 # ----- Data -----
16
17 m = 5.48e-4
18 h2 = (6.58e-16)**2
19 E0 = 1
20 dx=0.01
21
22 # ----- Set the x axis -----
```

```
23
24  x = arange(0,6,dx)
25
26  # ----- Potential barrier -----
27
28  def V(x):
29      if (x > 2 and x < 3):
30          y=20
31      else:
32          y=0
33      return y
34
35  # ----- Function to generate the wave function
36  #    Returns the wave function and error at x=6
37
38  def psiend(p):
39  E=p
40  global fa
41  f=[E] ; f.append(E)
42  for i in range(1,len(x)-1):
43      f[i] = (2 - (dx**2)*(2*m/h2)*1.362e-28*(E-V(x
        [i])))*f[i-1]-f[i-2]
44      f.append(f[i])
45      fa = asarray(f)
46      error = f[599]
47      return error
48
49  #    Iterate E until psi(x=6)=0
50  E = fsolve(psiend,(E0))
51
52  print("E=",E)
53
54  # ----- Normalize the psi function and plot -----
55
56  fa = fa/(sum(fa*fa))**0.5
57  import matplotlib.pyplot as plt
58  pdf = fa*fa
```

```
59 fig = plt.figure(1)
60 plt.plot(x,pdf)
61
62 # ----- Plot the wave function -----
63 fig = plt.figure(2)
64 plt.plot(x,fa,[0,2,2.001,3,3.001,6],[0,0,max(fa),
     max(fa),0,0])
65 plt.title('Wave function $\Psi$')
66 plt.xlabel('Distance, uma')
```

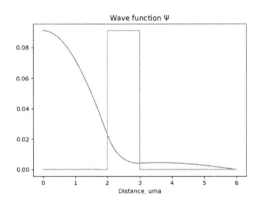

7.5   Answer to *Listen to that Whale!*

```python
# -*- coding: utf-8 -*-
"""
Created on Wed Jun 20 18:12:55 2018

@author: jrg
"""

# -*- coding: utf-8 -*-
"""
Created on Tue Jun 19 09:34:53 2018

@author: JRG

This script obtains a spectrum of a sound (wav).
In order to reduce aliasing, a Hann window is
    applied
to data vs time, and then a fast Fourier
transform to obtain a frequency decomposition.

"""

from scipy.io import wavfile
import numpy as np
from matplotlib import pyplot as plt
import os

# ----- Read the wav file -----

filein = 'whale1a.wav' # 717 y 915 Hz
samplerate, data = wavfile.read(filein)
N = len(data)

#os.system('start '+filein)

```

75

```
34 # ----- set a times axis, for plotting -----
35
36 times = np.arange(len(data))/float(samplerate)
37 dt=times[1]-times[0]
38
39 # ----- Plot the wave -----
40
41 plt.close('all')
42 plt.figure(1)
43 plt.plot(times, data)
44 plt.title('Time Domain Signal')
45 plt.xlabel('Time, s')
46 plt.ylabel('Amplitude ($Unit$)')
47
48 # ----- Set and apply a Hann window -----
49
50 hann = np.hanning(len(data))
51 data_hann = hann*data   # apply Hann
52
53 # ----- Perform FFT -----
54
55 YY = np.fft.fft(data_hann) # Calc FFT
56 f = np.linspace(0, samplerate, N, endpoint=True)
57
58 # ----- Normalize to /N -----
59 YYnorm = YY*2/N
60
61 # ----- Discard 2nd half -----
62
63 fhalf = f[:int(N/2)]
64 YYnormhalf = YYnorm[:int(N/2)]
65
66 # ----- Plot spectrum -----
67
68 plt.figure(2)
69 plt.plot(fhalf, abs(YYnormhalf))
70 plt.title('Frequency Domain Signal')
```

```
71 plt.xlabel('Frequency ($Hz$)')
72 plt.ylabel('Amplitude ($Unit$)')
73
74 # ----- Print some results-----
75
76 print("\nAnalysis of "+filein)
77 print('number of data N=',N)
78 print('Sampling dt=',dt)
79 print('Fmin Hz=',fhalf[0],' Fmax Hz=',fhalf[-1])
```

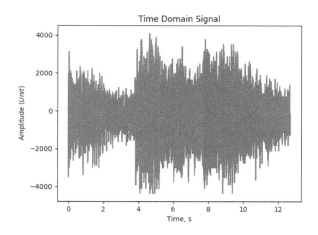

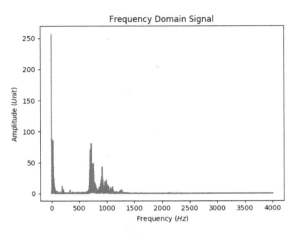

Figure 7.3: Whale calling in the time and frequency domain. Two peaks emerge at 717 Hz and 915 Hz.

7.6 Answer to *Calculate π with Montecarlo*

```
1  # -*- coding: utf-8 -*-
2  """
3  Created on Tue Jun 19 20:24:47 2018
4
5  Script to estimate PI with Montecarlo
6
7  @author: JRG
8  """
9
10 from numpy import random
11
12 # ----- bounding box -----
13
```

```
14  x1 , x2= -1, 1
15  y1 , y2= -1, 1
16
17
18  # ----- generate x,y samples -----
19
20  n=200000 ; sum=0
21  x_sample = random.uniform(x1, x2, n)
22  y_sample = random.uniform(y1, y2, n)
23
24  for i in range(0,n):
25      x=x_sample[i]
26      y=y_sample[i]
27
28  # ----- check if x,y inside bounds -----
29
30  if (x**2 + y**2 < 1):
31      inside = 1
32      else: inside = 0
33
34  # ----- accumulate function when inside -----
35  fun = 1
36  sum = sum + fun*inside
37
38  I_montec=sum/n*(x2-x1)*(y2-y1)
39
40  print('PI_Montecarlo = ',I_montec)
```

```
PI_Montecarlo =   3.1447
```

79

A   Python Primer

This part is devoted to those readers that have very little or no knowledge about Python as a programming language. I have had the opportunity to verify that people with real interest in something build knowledge from concrete information, they apply an inductive method. Taking into account this reality, I have taught computer languages giving only relevant pieces of information for the reader to learn and not get bored. On many occasions, providing a small introduction or some clues on where to start, is enough so that the learner can walk freely.

In the following lines, Python will be presented in a few brushstrokes, basic claculations, how to write and execute a script, and things like that. Of course, if the reader already has knowledge of this language, he or she can avoid this appendix without hesitation.

The basics

Python is a programming language for high level scripts with very interesting features: simplicity, power, and versatility. Its creator (Guido van Rossum) emphasized that the scripts were legible and well structured.

It is a powerful and fashionable language like Java or C very extended in academic environments and companies, but far more intuitive and simple. It can be used for web development, GUI development, scientific and numerical calculation, software development and operative systems administration.

Generally, Python is cross-platform. It can be executed in Windows, Linux, and macOS. Orders and sentences can be executed interactively in console mode, or they can be stored and executed in a *.py script file. Console mode is very useful to test instructions before writing them in the script.

There is a lot of information (tutorials, manuals, user groups, examples on the internet, ...). The code, utilities, manuals, online console window, libraries, ... are at www.python.org. Besides, you will find very good description in https://es.wikipedia.org/wiki/Python.

Running Python

Today, there is a number of suites that greatly facilitate writing and running Python. For MS-Windows, I recommend the Anaconda/Spyder IDE, which is an integrated development environment for the Python language. The suite is is developed and distributed under the MIT license, it is multi-platform and free.

Anaconda/Spyder integrates useful libraries (modules) such as NumPy, SciPy, and Matplotlib, and it gives easy access to many others like Tkinter, Pandas,...

Basically, it shows three windows: (1) editing, (2) scanning of variables and files, and (3) execution console. Do you want to run your first script? See Figure A.1.

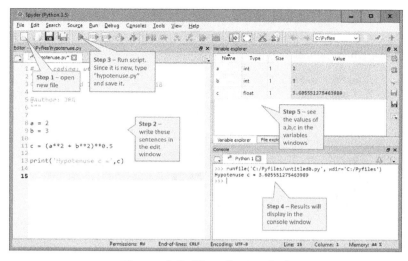

Figure A.1: Your first script!

Assignment of variables

Variables can be any combination of characters and numbers, uppercase, and lower case. Assigned values can be reals or floats, integers, complex, character chains or strings, etc.

```
 1  # This line is a comment
 2
 3  """
 4    This block is a LONG COMMENT. It is
 5    bounded between triple quote marks. Note
 6    that the sintax of Python is easy yet powerful,
 7    and easy to read.
 8    It is recommended to start the script
 9    with key information such  as the name of the
10    script, author, version of Python, use,
11    restrictions, as well as any other information
12    that facilitates the reading.
```

83

```
13  """
14
15  mass = 36.12        # a real number (float)
16
17  gravity = 9.81      # another real number
18
19  jas = 32            # an integer
20
21  alpha = 2 + 3j      # a complex number
22
23  beta = complex(2,3) # alternate definition of
        complex
24
25  My_name = "Wonder123_4dogs" # alphanumeric string
26
```

Assignment of lists and arrays

Lists of numbers and alphanumeric strings can be created easily. Arrays are like vector and matrix structures, and they can be operated in algebraic operations as numbers. Before using arrays, you need to import numpy library.

```
1   my_list = [2, 3, 5, 8]  # This is a list
2
3   from numpy import array
4
5   vec = array([1,4,6])      # This is an array
6
7   # Column array
8   vec_col = array([1,2,3]).reshape(-1,1)
9
10  # Column array
11  vec_col1 = array([[1],[2],[3]])
12
13   # Column array, more visual
```

```
14 vec_col2 =   array([[1],
15                     [2],
16                     [3]])
17
18  # Matrix
19 mat = array([[1,2,6], [3,4,9],[1,-2,7]])
20
21 # Matrix, more visual
22 mat1 = array([[1,2,6],
23               [3,4,9],
24               [1,-2,7]])
25
```

There are other useful data structures like
tuple, and dictionary. You may refer to a Python manual.

Calculations and operations

You can perform all sort of mathematical operations with data.
They can be reals, integers, text chains, etc.

```
1
2 from scipy import *
3 from numpy import *
4
5 force = mass * gravity
6
7 alpha = log((sin(pi*gravity))**2)-0.5
8
9 Ux3 = pi*sin(alpha)*e
10
11 Vec2 = vec * vec
12
13 Vec3 = vec2 * 2/3
14
15 Mat3 = mat1 * mat1
16
```

```
17 Au = linalg.eigvals(mat1)
18
19 your_name = "hello "+ My_name + "abc"
```

Extract data from arrays

Very powerful syntax. Note that array indexing starts in 0, not in 1.

```
1
2 aa = vec[2]     # extract 3d coordinate of array
3
4 bb = vec[0:2]  # extract from 1st to 3rd
     coordinate
5
6 cc = vec[:]     # extract all
7
8 Evec = mat1[:,1]  # extract 2nd column
9
```

Functions

A very useful feature of Python is the possibility od defining functions. This a good strategy when you need to execute a series of sentences that can be arranged in a callable structure. Besides, they add clearness to the reading. Functions can have any number of inputs and outputs as seen in the following examples.

```
1 # Example with one input, one output
2
3 def conductivity(t):
4     a = 2150
5     b =  1.05
```

86

```
6    y = a + b/((t+273)-73.15)
7    return y
```

```
1  # Example with two inputs, three outputs
2
3  def hipot(x,y):
4      z = (x**2 + y**2)**0.5
5      l = x + y + z
6      v = x*y*z*l
7      return z,l,v
```

Once they have been declared, they can be call downstream in the script, in the same way as any other intrinsic function.

```
1
2  T = conductivity(2200) / 235.12
3
4  gamma = 6.12*hipot(2,3)
5
```

Everything that has been declared inside a function is local. To become accessible you need to include it in the `return` sentence, or declare it as `global`. However, variable that have been declared out of the function bounds is accessible from the inside.

Importing modules (libraries)

There are many libraries in Python that allow you to perform calculations in different areas. Some of the most useful are `scipy`, `numpy`, and `matplotlib`, and they are included in the Anaconda package, so you only need to import the library in the script.

In order to see which modules are installed, open a command prompt and type "> pip list". If you need a module that is not installed, open a command prompt and type "> pip modulename". Check *https://docs.python.org/3/py-modindex.html* for a list of available modules.

You can import an entire module or only a portion of it. You will find different practices on the Internet. We can simplify up to four modes of importing a molule:

```
1  # 1 - Not bad, it imports the entire module
2  from numpy import *
3
4  # 2 - Import only a specific function
5  from numpy import array
6
7  # 3 - Import the entire module
8  import numpy
9
10 # 4 - Import the module and rename it
11 import numpy as np  # 4 - import and rename it
12
```

Calling a portion depends on how we imported the module

```
1
2  g = array([1,2])     # First and second method
3  g = numpy.array([1,2])  # Third method
4  g = np.array ([1,2,]) # Fourth method
5
```

Loops

Scripts often need some internal controls. In this section we see examples of while, for, and if/then/else loops. Note that all sentences inside a loop are indented, four spaces per looping level

88

```
1
2 #     While loop ---------------------
3 i = 0
4     while i < 5:
5     print(i)  # print numbers from 0 to 4
6     i = i+1   # i +=1 is an alternative
7
8 #     for loop ------------------------
9 for i in (0,1,2,3,4): # for i in range(4) is an
       alternative
10    print (i)  # print numbers from 0 to 4
11
12 #    if/then/else loop --------------
13 a=1 ; b = 2
14 if a==b:
15    print('They are identical')
16 else:
17    print ("No, they are different")
18
```

Plotting 2D arrays

```
1 #   First, we prepare the data
2
3 x1 = array([2.1 ,3.2, 6, 9.5, 10, 12])
4 y1 = array([4.1, 6., 37, 70, 92,100])
5
6 #   Then, we plot and label
7 import matplotlib.pyplot as plt # import plotting
       module
8
9 plt.close('all') # Let us close all previous
       plots
10 fig = plt.figure(1) # number the figure
11 plt.plot(x1,y1,'g-o', x1, y1*2,'r--x')
```

89

```
12
13 plt.title('Plot of x1 versus y1')
14 plt.legend(('y1','2*y1'))
15 plt.xlabel('x1, meters')
16 plt.ylabel('y1, pounds')
```

Note that the type of connections between data points is controlled with 'g-o' (green/line/circle) and 'r–x' (red/dash/x). There are many combinations of colors, lines, and marks. See Python manual for options.

Plotting 3D arrays

```
1  # Let us prepare data
2
3  from numpy import array
4  x1 = array([2.1 ,3.2, 6, 9.5, 10, 12])
5  y1 = array([4.1, 6., 37, 70, 92,100])
6  z1 = array([6., 6., 9., 15., 14., 13.])
7
8  # Now, we plot the 3D line
9  from mpl_toolkits.mplot3d import Axes3D
10 import matplotlib.pyplot as plt
11
12 fig = plt.figure(2)
13 ax = plt.axes(projection='3d')
14 ax.plot(x1, y1, z1, '-o')
15
16 plt.title('Example of 3D line plot')
17 plt.xlabel('x1 values')
18 plt.ylabel('y1 values')
19
20
```

Contour plot

```
# Let us prepare data

from numpy import arange, meshgrid
from scipy import exp

# Generate high resolution x and y axis
x= arange(-2,2,.05)
y= arange(-2,2,.05)

# Generate a xx*yy mesh
xx,yy = meshgrid(x,y)

# Assign zz for each mesh point
zz = xx*exp(-xx**2 - yy**2)

# Now you can plot
from matplotlib.pyplot import contourf, colorbar
fig = plt.figure(3)
contourf(xx,yy,zz)
colorbar()
plt.title('Example of 3D contour plot')
plt.xlabel('xx values')
plt.ylabel('yy values')
```

Plotting a 3D surface

```
# ... continuation of script
import matplotlib.pyplot as plt
from matplotlib.pyplot import axes, contourf,
    colorbar
from mpl_toolkits.mplot3d import Axes3D

fig = plt.figure(4)
ax = plt.axes(projection='3d')
```

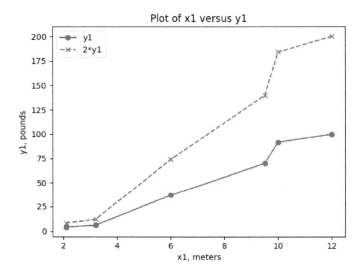

```
8 ax.plot_surface(xx, yy, zz, cmap=plt.cm.jet,
     rstride=1, cstride=1, linewidth=0)
9
10 plt.title('Example of 3D surface plot')
11 plt.xlabel('xx values')
12 plt.ylabel('yy values')
```

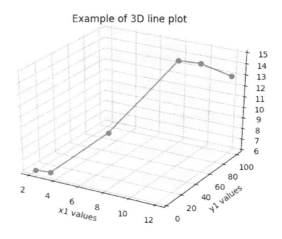

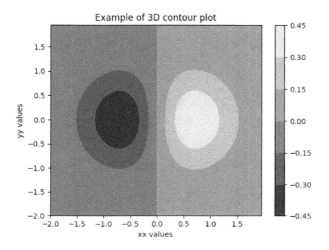

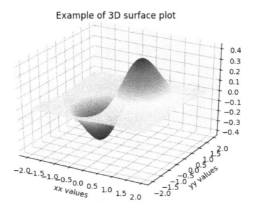

Example of 3D surface plot

Read data from text files

First, we read the entire file and store it in a list

```
1 arch1 = open("data.txt","r")  # r stands for read
2 lineas = arch1.readlines()
3 arch1.close
```

Once the file has been read and stored in 'lineas' we can search inside, extract values, and so on. Some interesting things to do are:

```
1 # Count the number of lines
2 Lon = len(lineas)
3
4 # Read text in line 3, columns 0 to 38
5 A = lineas[3][0:38]
6
7 # Read float number in line 3, columns 3 to 15
```

```
 8 AA = float(lineas[12][3:15])
 9
10 # Find line with with a specific text
11 i=0 ; click=0
12 for i in range(Lon-1):
13     if click==0 and ("right to live" in lineas[i
       ]): ilin=i ; click=1
14
15 # Extract lists of values X and Y
16 X,Y = [],[]
17 for i in range(12,19): # between lines 12 and 19
18     X.append( float( lineas[i][1:5] ))   # columns
       1 to 5
19     Y.append( float( lineas[i][6:12] )) # columns
       6 to 12
```

In the previous example, you need to know in advance the line numbers that include your data. But, if you already know that numbers are in fields 0 and 1, the last two lines are simplified:

```
1     X.append( float( lineas[i].split()[0]))
2     Y.append( float( lineas[i].split()[1]))
```

Read data from txt file between some headers

Occasionally, your data are inside a file, between two headers. If you were to grab the data manually, first you should search for the begin header, descend to where data start actually, then copy all the data you need, and paste in a list or array. With Python this can be automatized greatly. You have to tell the code the same orders as you would do manually.

```
 1  #      1- Open, count, and read lines in file
 2  myfile = 'c:\pyfiles\filedata.txt'
 3  num_lines = sum(1 for line in open(myfile))
 4  with open(myfile) as f: lines = f.readlines()
 5
 6
 7  #      2- Find lines with begin and end headers
 8  click=0
 9  for i in range(num_lines-1):
10      if click==0 and ("begin text" in lines[i]):
11          istring1 = i; click=1
12      if click==1 and ("end text" in lines[i]):
13          istring2 = i ; click=2
14
15
16  #      3- Extract information in selected fields.
17  #          Sometimes you need to adjust lines
18  TIMEv=[]
19  VPWIv=[]
20  for linea in range(istring1+3 , istring2-2):
21
22      time= float(lines[linea].split()[0])
23      vol = float(lines[linea].split()[5])
24
25      TIMEv.append(time)
26      VPWIv.append(vol)
```

Read data from txt file with pure columns

If data are arranged in pure columns in a text file, the reading
is very simple. In the example below, data are stored in several
columns. We want to read data in columns 1,2, and 5.

```
1  arch2 = open("columns.txt", "r")
2  t,x,y = [],[],[]
3
4  for l in arch2:
5      row = l.split()
6      print(row)
7      t.append(float(row[0]))
8      x.append(float(row[1]))
9      y.append(float(row[5]))
10 arch2.close()
```

Read data from an Excel xls file

Something that is extremely useful when performing analysis is the possibility to read data from an Ms-Excel spreadsheet.

For cleanliness, in the example below we read only one value, the contents of cell 2D, but you can read complete ranges of cells both rows and columns. Remember that the first cell in Python is indexed as (0,0).

```
1  import xlrd
2
3  #    Open xls file and go to sheet 0
4  book = xlrd.open_workbook("data.xlsx")
5  first_sheet = book.sheet_by_index(0)
6
7  #    Extract value in cell 2D
8  valor = first_sheet.cell(1,3).value
```

Writing in text files

The Python sentence 'write', is used in order to write strings of alpha-numeric characters. If your data are float or integer numbers, you are ok. However, if they are combinations of numbers and characters, first you need to convert them into strings with 'str' sentence. The example below illustrates the different posibilities.

Note that, we can also add information to the end of a file by specificyng the option 'append' when opening the file.

```
arch1 = open("newfile1.txt", "w") # w - write, r
    - read, a - append

arch1.write("This is the first line\n")
arch1.write("and this is the second line.\n")
arch1.write('3.14\n')
arch1.write(str(mat))
arch1.close()
```

B | Packages Contents

Raw Python has a limited capability for Engineering and Science. However, there are great packages or libraries that extend the possibilities to almost any technical field. Very often, almost every week, the Python Users Community improves the components of these libraries or gives birth to new tools. In addition, the concept of programming objects and platforms for the development of operating systems has not been discussed in this book, but it is a fascinating area in continuous expansion.

The most important libraries from the scientific computing viewpoint are summarized in this Appendix.

Scipy

SciPy is an open source library of mathematical functions. The power of Python is greatly expanded with this suite. Some of the areas with dedicated routines are the following ones:

`https://www.scipy.org/`

- cluster - Clustering algorithms

- constants Physical and mathematical constants

- fftpack - Fast Fourier Transform routines

- terpolate - Interpolation and smoothing splines

- io - Input and Output

- linalg - Linear algebra

- maxentropy - Maximum entropy methods

- ndimage - N-dimensional image processing

- odr - Orthogonal distance regression

- optimize - Optimization and root-finding

- signal - Signal processing

- sparse - Sparse matrices and associated routines

- spatial - Spatial data structures and algorithms

- special - Special functions

- stats - Statistical distributions and functions

- weave - C/C++ integration

Numpy

NumPy is the fundamental package for scientific computing with Python. Some of the most interesting features are listed next.

`http://www.numpy.org/`

- Array creation routines

- Array manipulation routines

- Binary operations

- String operations

- C-Types Foreign Function Interface

- Datetime Support Functions

- Data type routines

- Linear algebra

- Mathematical functions with automatic domain

- Discrete Fourier Transform

- Financial functions

- Input and output

- Linear algebra (numpy.linalg)

- Logic functions

- Truth value testing

- Array contents

- Logical operations

- Mathematical functions

- Matrix library (numpy.matlib)

- Polynomials

- Random sampling

- Statistics

Other Packages

- **Matplotlib** - It is a versatile library to generate graphs and plots from the many different sources of data generated in Python.
  `https://matplotlib.org/`

- **Pandas** - This library is an extension to NumPy in order to handle data from a variety of sources, and to perform statistical analysis.
  `http://pandas.pydata.org/`

- **Sympy** - A library to expand the Python universe with symbolic handling of algebraic operations.
  `http://www.sympy.org/en/index.html`